# STEAM ON THE SOUTHERN
## A Colour Portfolio

**Roy Hobbs**

Ian Allan
60th
ANNIVERSARY

# Introduction

Although the smallest of the four companies formed as a result of the amalgamation of the numerous independent railways at the grouping of 1923, the Southern Railway nevertheless commanded an extremely important sector of the total system. This comprised, in the first instance, a particularly significant proportion of south-eastern commuter routes to London, these originating predominantly from the counties of Kent, Surrey and Sussex. Following the electrification of many main lines from these areas and the acceleration of services, coupled with the introduction of frequent interval timetabling, in mainly the inter-war years, the consequence was a vast expansion of housebuilding in these locations. This enabled many people to adopt the idea of living in country districts, or by the coast, providing an improved quality of life for those working in the metropolis. The company also inherited a considerable electrified suburban network, which had been developed, from the early 1900s, by its LBSCR and LSWR predecessors. This situation had been provoked by the advancement of the electric tram, with a marked loss of revenue on competing services.

Following amalgamation, the company also profited by inheriting the routes from several English Channel ports, especially those in Kent, connecting this country with the European continent, and through its principal terminal at Southampton, afforded the major link across the Atlantic to North America, with all the opportunities for trade that existed via this facility. Additionally, the company and its Southern Region successor had benefited until the 1960s from the vast amount of seasonal traffic generated to South Coast holiday resorts, particularly those in Kent, Sussex and Devon, along with the Isle of Wight.

Unfortunately, with changing lifestyles, including wider car ownership and a growing preference for foreign holidays, along with the expansion of aviation for both passenger and freight use, many of these services have declined, whilst a large number of coastal branches were closed during the 1960s.

With present uncertainties, however, it is rewarding, through the medium of colour photography, to drift back through the years and recall a period when one could still meander along

---

*Front cover:* In brilliant winter sunshine Maunsell 'S15' class 4-6-0 No 30837 climbs Medstead Bank with an LCGB railtour, marking the demise of the class, on 9 January 1966. This section of line, between Alton and Alresford, is now operated by the Mid-Hants Railway.

*Rear cover:* In August 1962 'A1X' class 0-6-0T No 32670 awaits clearance to enter the roadside tramway section of Newhaven's West Quay branch linking this to the main-line yard.

*Previous page:* Maunsell 'U1' class 2-6-0 No 31891 climbs the well-known Sole Street Bank, near Rochester, with an unidentified train from the Kent coast to London, in August 1958. The 'U1s' were a three-cylinder version of the designer's 'U' class of 1928, introduced as a direct result of rebuilding 'K1' class 2-6-4T No 890 (BR No 31890) following the 1927 Sevenoaks accident, when a two-cylinder 'K' class 2-6-4T derailed at speed. These were also subsequently rebuilt as the 'U' class, some 20 engines being converted.
*K. W. Wightman*
*All uncredited photos taken by the author.*

First published 2002

ISBN 0 7110 2841 9

Published by Ian Allan Publishing

an imprint of Ian Allan Publishing Ltd, Hersham, Surrey  KT12 4RG.
Printed by Ian Allan Printing Ltd, Hersham, Surrey  KT12 4RG.

Code:0205/B2

a Sussex branch line or travel on holiday to a Devon coastal resort behind the magic of steam traction. Occasions, it seemed, when the sun always shone and that these circumstances would remain for some considerable time to come.

Doubtless due to the ongoing electrification programme having been halted by World War 2, a large variety of steam locomotive types remained across the system in the post-war era, including several older examples operating on branch line and secondary duties. Despite the slow advance of early railway colour photography, it has still been found possible to illustrate the great majority of those classes working in the period from 1957 to 1967, whilst I have also endeavoured, as far as possible, to present a reasonably balanced overview of the system as a whole, including a variety of branches and main lines across the region, from Kent to Cornwall.

For those requiring additional information, many of the publications listed below have proved an invaluable reference source and are recommended for further study.

# Bibliography

F. Burtt: *LBSCR Locomotives* Ian Allan
F. Burtt: *LSWR Locomotives* Ian Allan
F. Burtt: *SECR Locomotives* Ian Allan
G. Daniels & L.A. Dench: *Passengers No More (3rd Edition)* Ian Allan
O.S. Nock: *Great Locomotives of the Southern Railway* Patrick Stephens
D. St. John Thomas & P.B. Whitehouse: *SR150: The Southern Railway* David & Charles
*A Regional History of the Railways of Great Britain* David and Charles
      Vol 1: D. St. John Thomas; *The West Country*
      Vol 2: H.P. White; *Southern England*
Other Publications : The various series published by the Middleton Press profiling the railways of Southern England.

Society Journals: RCTS *Railway Observer*, SLS *Bulletin*.
Magazines: *Railway Magazine*; *Steam Days*; *Trains Illustrated*.

# Acknowledgements

This publication contains predominantly the work of many other known and well-respected photographers of the railway scene during the period under review. To these I offer my grateful thanks for the loan of their often unique and valuable slides, without which this volume would be much the poorer. My particular appreciation goes especially to David Clark, now custodian of the work of the late Kenneth Wightman, to which he has kindly allowed access, and for his help in clarifying a number of points that arose whilst preparing the final text.

*Roy Hobbs*
Exeter
November 2001

*Above:* Seen here still in its unmodified form, prototype 'MN' class 4-6-2 No 35001 *Channel Packet* is shown near Shortlands with the 1.30pm down boat train on 22 June 1957. It is considerably altered from its initial appearance, when it also bore cast '21C1' cabside and 'Southern' tender plates. The locomotive was introduced in 1941 as the first of a 20-strong batch, these being identified as 'heavy goods and passenger locos' to circumvent wartime building restrictions. It survived, after August 1959 rebuilding, until withdrawal in November 1964. However, privately owned Nos 35005 *Canadian Pacific* and, until recently, 35028 *Clan Line,* both as rebuilt, remained operational on a variety of main-line excursions. *K.W. Wightman*

*Right:* Following the introduction of the 'Britannia' Class 7MT 4-6-2s in 1951, two of the class, Nos 70004 *William Shakespeare* and 70014 *Iron Duke*, were allocated to Stewarts Lane depot to work the prestigious continental 'Golden Arrow' Pullman service. The latter engine is seen with the down train, close to Shortlands Junction in April 1958, bearing the usual headboard and associated embellishments.*K. W. Wightman*

The former London, Chatham and Dover Railway (LCDR) main line was one of the original stamping grounds of Maunsell's 'King Arthur' class 4-6-0s, and No 30794 *Sir Ector de Maris* is shown here passing Ravensbourne station with a London to Ramsgate working on 21 July 1957. The 'N15s' were first brought into service on the LSWR by CME Robert Urie between 1918 and 1923, being a development of his 'H15' class mixed-traffic 4-6-0. Original numbering was 736-755 (BR Nos 30736-30755), and they were commonly known as 'Urie Arthurs'. Maunsell improved the design by modifying the front-end, and a further 10 engines were added in February 1925, (BR Nos 30448-30457), along with 30 built by the North British Locomotive Company (BR Nos 30763-30792), these being delivered the following May. The latter inevitably became known as 'Scotch Arthurs'. The great majority of these engines had bogie tenders from new, but 14 built at Eastleigh in 1926 and 1927 (BR Nos 30793-30806), were fitted with a shorter six-wheeled version, enabling them to use those turntables found on the Central (former LBSCR) Section. A few of Stewarts Lane's engines, once employed on the Continental boat trains, (BR Nos 30763-30772), were later fitted with the shorter type. Maunsell's modifications radically improved their performance, and they could subsequently be found over the whole SR system, especially the Kent Coast, West of England and Bournemouth services, prior to the introduction of Bulleid's Pacifics. *K. W. Wightman*

'D1' class 4-4-0 No 31749 is shown departing Bromley South with an excursion for the Kent coast on 23 June 1957. The 'D1' 4-4-0s were Maunsell rebuilds of Wainwright's 'D' class, the first of these taking place in 1921. The original boiler barrel was retained and a new Belpaire firebox installed. At the same time a Maunsell superheater was fitted, boiler pressure increased from 175 to 180psi and piston valves replaced the original slide valves. In all 21 engines were so modified, providing marked improvements in performance compared with the original design. No 31749, the last withdrawn, was among 10 examples rebuilt by Beyer Peacock in Manchester. *K. W. Wightman*

Hither Green MPD is shown in this view, taken on 27 March 1959, with a variety of locos present, including ex-SECR 'C' class and Bulleid 'Q1' class 0-6-0s, Maunsell 'W' class 2-6-4Ts and a solitary 'King Arthur' class 4-6-0, No 30806 *Sir Galleron*. Concerned mainly with freight operation, the depot maintained No 30806 in prime external condition to work one rush-hour duty from Cannon Street. Inter-regional freight traffic across London was amongst its main tasks, and it also received visits from former GNR 0-6-2T and 0-6-0T classes from Ferme Park (ER) and LMR '3F' 0-6-0Ts from Brent (LMR) sidings. These worked goods traffic over the Metropolitan Railway Widened Lines via Faringdon and Blackfriars. Opened in 1933 by the Southern Railway, the depot closed to steam in November 1961 when the Class 33 diesels took over. However, a few 'C' class 0-6-0s were retained for special duties for a time. *R. C. Riley*

At Gravesend Central on 24 September 1960, 'Q1' class 0-6-0 No 33037 is shown with an unidentified duty for the Allhallows line, whilst sister engine No 33036 waits with its pre-Grouping auto set to undertake a later branch service. These engines were used, from time to time, alongside the former SECR 'H' class 0-4-4Ts normally allocated to such workings. Employment of the 'Q1's probably arose from shortages at Tonbridge depot. *T. B. Owen*

*Above:* 'L' class 4-4-0 No 31779 approaches Faversham with an up working from Dover, two days prior to electrification, on 15 June 1959. Faversham locomotive depot, lying in the fork between the Margate and Dover lines, can be seen above the last few carriages of the train. The class was introduced in 1914 during Maunsell's reign on the SECR, the basic design being prepared under Wainwright's direction. No 31764 entered Ashford Works during April 1961 to be restored for excursion use, though plans were later abandoned.
*R. C. Riley*

*Right:* The last remaining members of the former SECR 'O1' class 0-6-0s were retained specifically to work the final remnant of the East Kent Light Railway (EKLR) from Shepherdswell to Tilmanstone Colliery, due to the lightness of the permanent way. This line was one of those originally constructed by Colonel Stephens of light railway fame. The 'O1' class originated as rebuilds by Wainwright of James Stirling's 'O' class of 1878, being updated with an 'H' class domed boiler and 'C' class style cab, commencing 1903. In their rebuilt form they still retained the distinctive outside sprung tender, which made them readily identifiable from their similar 'C' class sisters, whilst they were also some $2\frac{1}{2}$ tons lighter. A member of the original 'O' class, SECR No 98, was used, well into the 1950s, as a steam-heating boiler at Ramsgate carriage sidings. The example illustrated, No 31258, is shown at Shepherdswell on 23 May 1959 prior to working an enthusiasts special to Tilmanstone Colliery. The van included in the train make up is to hold participants' bicycles, enabling photography *en route*!
*T. B. Owen*

*Left:* Illustrated here is an example of the SECR 'R1' class 0-6-0T, No 31047, at its home depot of Folkestone on 28 June 1959. The type was introduced on the SER by James Stirling in 1888 as Class R specifically for shunting duties, being confined mainly to the Kent area. However, they also saw passenger use on the Whitstable and Elham Valley branches. Wainwright later rebuilt 13 as Class R1, fitting them with his standard domed boiler and so-called 'Pagoda' cab. Those that were retained for the Whitstable branch kept the rounded Stirling cab and were fitted with chimneys of a reduced height, enabling them to negotiate the restricted Tyler Hill Tunnel. The class was particularly associated with the steeply graded Folkestone Harbour branch, where they were often used in triplicate — two on the head end and one banking at the rear. On some occasions a quadruple formation even became necessary. For these duties some of the engines employed were fitted with an additional sandbox in front of the driving wheels. The examples used here survived the longest, being replaced by WR 0-6-0PTs in 1959. *T. B. Owen*

*Above:* Against the background of chalk downland bordering the English Channel coast, we find 'Battle of Britain' class 4-6-2 No 34086 *219 Squadron* approaching Folkestone Junction with an up boat train from Dover on 4 April 1959. The lines diverging on the right-hand side of the picture are those to Folkestone Harbour. Trains from London would reverse at this point, where banking engines would take over. By this time, these duties were handled by the former WR 0-6-0PTs, one of which is visible in the exchange sidings. *R. C. Riley*

In this view, taken from the steps of Tonbridge 'B' signalbox, 'H' class 0-4-4T No 31329 is observed with the empty coaching stock of a Maidstone West to Tonbridge auto service on 26 October 1957. A strengthening coach, in carmine and cream livery, has been included in the usual Maunsell two-coach push-pull set. The 66 'H' class engines were constructed between 1904 and 1915 to the designs of Wainwright, being a replacement for Stirling's similar 'Q1' class 0-4-4Ts, and intended for use on increasingly heavy suburban traffic. When new these engines were painted in fully lined-out green passenger livery, and were the first to have individually cut brass figures on the cab sides. This engine, as No 329, was used in both 1904 and 1926 for oil-firing experiments. Following the Grouping the class was later adapted for use in conjunction with push-pull units over both the former SECR and LBSCR lines and branches, and could be seen on these duties well into the BR era, lasting until the end of steam on Three Bridges to Tunbridge Wells workings in 1964, for example. *K. W. Wightman*

14

Getting to grips with its train, as it passes under Tonbridge station bridge with a Hastings-line freight on 12 October 1957, we see Wainwright 'C' class 0-6-0 No 31590, which could be considered as the standard goods loco of the SECR. Introduced in 1900, the class eventually totalled 109 examples, and replaced Stirling's earlier and less powerful 'O' class, in many cases on a one for one basis. The locomotives differed in appearance from these, to which they were otherwise quite similar, by the addition of balance weights in the driving wheels.

As delivered they were painted in Wainwright's striking lined green passenger livery, which colour scheme can be seen today on No 592 (BR No 31592) currently on the Bluebell Railway. One engine, No 685 (BR No 31685), was rebuilt as an 0-6-0ST ('S' class) by Maunsell in 1917 to evaluate increases in available adhesive weight. Despite being mainly goods engines, the 'C' class could often be seen on all kinds of passenger duties, including main-line excursions together with branch and secondary-line work. *K. W. Wightman*

*Left:* Shown on the route with which the class was associated for many years, 'Schools' 4-4-0 No 30901 *Winchester* is seen with the 12.16pm Charing Cross to Hastings working (Duty 146), near Wadhurst, on 15 June 1957. The route was particularly difficult, with many notable gradients, curves and tunnels, but the 'Schools' proved masters of the task from their introduction in 1930 until completion of route dieselisation in 1958, following which they were dispersed to other services. Hastings-line tunnels were narrower than normal, arising from the contractor's negligence in failing to provide sufficient brick linings and filling, as originally specified. Following the collapse of Mountfield Tunnel in 1855, these were all subsequently relined, reducing width and requiring the operation of passenger stock with a specially narrow profile. However, during the 1986 electrification, single track was installed in four tunnels, allowing the use of conventional electric units. *C. Hogg*

*Right:* Departing Wadhurst with a Hastings stopping service in the same month, Maunsell 'L1' class 4-4-0 No 31786 is shown coupled to one of the ex-SECR Birdcage Triple sets, then commonly in use for such services on the Eastern and Central Sections of the Southern Region. The 'L1' class locomotives were brought into service from 1926, and were the culmination of SECR 4-4-0 design, being basically a development of Wainwright's 'L' class of 1914 with certain front-end improvements, incorporating experience gained from the operation of the 'N' class 2-6-0s. They proved extremely successful in service, and were regularly used on a variety of work in the Kent area, including express and secondary main-line duties. *K. W. Wightman*

*Left:* The SECR equivalent of the LBSCR's famous 'A1X' class 'Terrier' 0-6-0Ts, the 'P' class, were built in 1909/10 especially to operate various rail motor workings, one of these being the long-closed branch to Greenwich Park running originally from Nunhead, along with similar services between Otford and Sevenoaks and Reading to Ash. Not being particularly successful in this role they were eventually demoted to other tasks, including those of shed pilots and shunting duties in restricted locations. They were only eight in number, and precisely half have survived into preservation. The example illustrated, formerly No 31556, was purchased by Hodson, Flour Millers of Robertsbridge, and is shown here at its home base in May 1965. It has since been taken over by the KESR Society at Tenterden, and restored to original lined SECR livery and earlier identity as No 753.

*Above:* An interesting view of 'L' class 4-4-0 No 31777, with a six-coach train from Redhill to Tonbridge at Bough Beech on a beautiful spring day, 31 May 1958, and on a route commonly associated with these 4-4-0s. Coaching stock consists of an ex-SECR Birdcage Triple set plus a rake of Maunsell vehicles in the carmine and cream main-line livery and an unidentified van. *K. W. Wightman*

*Above:* As well as their normal goods duties, Billinton's 'K' class 2-6-0s could often be found during postwar summer periods on a variety of inter-regional trains such as the Hastings to Wolverhampton service, between Brighton and Redhill, and those travelling via Clapham Junction and the West London line. No 32342 is seen leaving Kensington (Olympia) with the 12.30pm Hastings to Manchester on 22 August 1959. *K. W.Wightman*

*Right:* As with the 'K' class, the few remaining Brighton Atlantics could also be found during the 1950s working the various inter-regional trains which used the

West London Extension lines to Willesden. Here we see the last survivor, 'H2' class 4-4-2 No 32424 *Beachy Head*, approaching Clapham Junction with one of the successors to the prewar 'Sunny South Express', running from Leicester to Brighton, on 25 August 1957. Showing obvious signs of lineage with the GNR Atlantics, the 'H1' series was first introduced by LBSCR Chief Engineer D. Earle Marsh in 1905 and, together with the six comprising the 'H2' class of 1911, totalled 11 engines. At the time of writing, the Bluebell Railway is contemplating building a replica, having acquired a surviving GNR Atlantic boiler. *K. W. Wightman*

*Left:* Norwood Junction locomotive depot, built in 1933, is seen here in this general view taken from the access footbridge on 13 April 1960. Despite the intrusion of diesel shunters by this time, a variety of Brighton engines are still evident, examples of 'E2', 'K' and 'C2X' classes being present along with one of Maunsell's Moguls. The depot was also home to several of Maunsell's 'W' class 2-6-4Ts, which handled the inter-regional freight-transfer traffic from the large local marshalling yard. Its situation was within a triangle formed by the main London Bridge to Brighton and Crystal Palace to Beckenham Junction lines and a steep spur descending from the latter to Norwood Junction station. This is shown on the right-hand side. Following demolition in 1966, the site became a BR engineering base. *R. C. Riley*

*Above:* The 'C2X' class 0-6-0s, totalling some 45 examples, were rebuilds from 1908 by Marsh of Billinton's 'C2' class of 1893, the final two being modified at Ashford as late as 1940 in SR days. The larger replacement boiler allowed these engines to cope with the increasing loads of the time. A number were allocated to Norwood Junction, No 32521 and a sister loco being seen here on 3 August 1959. *R. C. Riley*

Rebuilt 'Battle of Britain' class 4-6-2 No 34089 *602 Squadron* approaches East Croydon station with the 6.10pm evening commuter working from Victoria to Brighton via Oxted, Uckfield and Lewes in June 1962. A few of the heavier trains from London termini, during the afternoon rush-hour period, were often worked by larger engines other than the BR Standard '4MT' class 2-6-4Ts, which normally monopolised trains over the Oxted lines at this time in the pre-dieselisation era. Another notable working during the period was the 4.48pm from London Bridge, which divided at the little country station of Ashurst. This was regularly hauled by a Maunsell 'U1' class 2-6-0, which continued forward to Brighton with the front portion, whilst the remaining coaches were taken on to Tunbridge Wells, usually by a 'Q' class 0-6-0. Dieselisation of Oxted lines services was virtually complete by September 1963, when one Saturday diagram remained. Electrification of the Sanderstead to East Grinstead section followed in October 1987, leaving only the Hurst Green to Uckfield route to be converted. No 34089 was originally constructed at the former LBSCR works in Brighton during December 1948. Rebuilding took place at Eastleigh in November 1960, with withdrawal occuring in July 1967, when the steam era on the Southern Region finally drew to a close.

The winter of 1963 proved to be more severe than those of several years previously, and, in the characteristic snowy landscape, former SECR 'H' class 0-4-4T No 31005 departs Edenbridge Town in February with an Oxted to Tunbridge Wells West motor working. With subsequent line closures the section from Hurst Green Junction to Eridge became linked with that from Eridge to Uckfield, forming one continuous branch. This is currently DEMU operated. The Oxted & Groombridge Railway of 1881 was opened from Hurst Green to Edenbridge on 2 January 1888, extending to Ashurst Junction on 1 October 1888.

*Below:* In this scene, near Groombridge, 'Schools' class 4-4-0 No 30934 *St. Lawrence* is shown on 1 July 1961 with the 11.55am Brighton to Tonbridge train, comprising a rake of Maunsell narrow slab-sided stock suitable for the Hastings-line tunnels. No 30934, as indicated by the wide chimney, was one of the 21 fitted by Bulleid with the Lemaitre multi-jet blastpipe, resulting from the improved performance of the 'Lord Nelson' class following this modification. After the 1958 dieselisation of the London to Hastings services on which the 'Schools' had reigned supreme, and with the subsequent electrification of the remaining Kent lines, they were transferred away to other locations for working various secondary duties. A section of line between Eridge and Tunbridge Wells is now with preservationists. *C. Hogg*

*Right:* One of the LBSCR's maids of all work, 'E4' class 0-6-2T No 32474 takes water at Polegate whilst working a short freight on 18 May 1962. It was amongst the last of this class, being first withdrawn in the notorious BR steam purge of December 1962. However, a shortage of diesel shunters led to a return to service in January 1963 along with two other 'E4s', final withdrawal taking place in May 1963. *D. B. Clark*

*Left:* Here 'W' class 2-6-4T No 31920 is shown at Lingfield having arrived with a banana train on 1 June 1963. The 15 examples, built in 1931, were designed specifically for cross London inter-regional freight transfer work, and utilised parts from 'River' class 2-6-4Ts, rebuilt following the 1927 Sevenoaks accident. A number ended their days on Exeter banking duties in 1963. *D. B. Clark*

*Above:* A view here of Sheffield Park station on the East Grinstead to Lewes line, taken in BR days prior to the first closure on 29 May 1955. This was later found illegal and the line re-opened from August 1956 to March 1958 when final BR closure took effect. The station is now widely known as the southern terminus of the Bluebell Railway. Though the character of the station remains, the goods yard area has undergone a complete transformation since services restarted in 1960. This now incorporates a newly constructed loco works and running shed, together with similar public restaurant and bookshop facilities. The train shown is the 3.35pm Oxted to Brighton on 30 April 1955, featuring ex-SECR Birdcage Triple Set No 596 headed by Fairburn Class 4MT 2-6-4T No 42081. *R. C. Riley*

*Above:* Against the backdrop of the North Downs, and having passed Merstham station, 'N' class 2-6-0 No 31834 heads south with an evening van train for Kent via Redhill during October 1963. The M25 motorway now runs roughly parallel to the North Downs, passing under both this and Quarry avoiding line, just to the north of the station.

*Right:* A beautifully clean 'N1' class Mogul No 31877, presumably ex-works after overhaul, passes Redhill depot with a Tonbridge-bound working on

15 August 1959. This is possibly the 5.08pm from Redhill, to which Duty 293 applied in 1958. The 'N1' class, totalling six engines, was a three-cylinder version of Maunsell's 'N' class, and the first, later No 31822, appeared in SECR days in 1922, the remainder following in 1930. They were constructed primarily for use on the Tonbridge to Hastings route, where a narrower width over cylinders permitted their use, as compared to the 'Ns' which were unable to negotiate the restricted clearances. All were taken out of service in 1962.
*K. W. Wightman*

*Left:* BR Standard Class 4MT 4-6-0 No 75067 approaches Redhill Tunnel on the Quarry avoiding line, with a northbound inter-regional holiday train from the South Coast on 24 August 1963. Several Standard classes were produced by BR from 1951 on, a number being based on earlier LMS types. However, that illustrated was an original design, being a lighter version of the BR Class 5MT 4-6-0 with wider route availability.

*Above:* Foreign visitors to the Brighton line were no strangers, LMR 'Black 5' 4-6-0s regularly working post-war excursions to various South Coast resorts,

especially on summer weekends. In addition, during the wartime period until around 1948, a regular freight trip, variously using LMSR '4F' 0-6-0s, 'Super D' 0-8-0s, 'Crab' 2-6-0s and '8F' 2-8-0s, operated between Willesden and Three Bridges yard. There was an apparent precedent here, as a similar working had existed in the inter-war years. However, an exceptional duty on 4 June 1965 found LMR Class 8F 2-8-0 No 48544 of Bletchley (1E) shed in charge of a Newcastle to Hove 20-van pigeon special, plus support coach. It is seen at Haywards Heath taking water for the onward journey. *D. B. Clark*

*Above:* One of Stroudley's famous 'Terriers', 'A1X' class 0-6-0T No 32636, along with 'E6' class 0-6-2T No 32418, waits at Brighton shed on 7 October 1962 to take over the RCTS 'Sussex Coast' railtour for the return trip to Seaford. No 32636 is better known as *Fenchurch*, and for being allocated to Newhaven for use on the West Quay branch, which it worked continuously between 1898 and 1955. It now resides on the Bluebell Railway, having been restored to near 'A1' condition with shortened smokebox and numbered 672. No 32418 was one of 12 engines introduced by R. J. Billinton in 1904 for goods duties, that shown being, with BR No 32417, one of the last two built. The original intention had been to construct both in eight-coupled form, but this proposal was cancelled by his

successor, D. Earle Marsh. They were the last examples in BR service, both being withdrawn in December 1962.

*Right:* Seen on Brighton shed is 'N15X' class 4-6-0 No 32329 *Stephenson*, having brought an SLS special from London Bridge on 23 June 1956. The class were rebuilds from 1934 of the seven LBSCR 'L' class 4-6-4Ts, employed until electrification on Brighton expresses. Then redundant, they were converted for use in the Nine Elms 'King Arthur' link, though proving none too successful in this role. All were withdrawn by July 1957. *R. C. Riley*

'Q' class 0-6-0 No 30547 carries out a shunting movement at Southwater during May 1962, on the line between Christ's Hospital (Itchingfield Junction) and Horsham, shortly before goods operation on this stretch of line came to an end. The particular source of revenue here was Southwater brickworks, the chimneys of which are evident to the rear of this view. Their own siding can be seen diverging right, at the rear of the train. Passenger traffic continued until 7 March 1966, when line closure took place apart from a short section at the southern end, retained to serve Beeding cement works. Services were latterly operated by the Ivatt Class 2MT 2-6-2Ts of LMS design, these having taken over from the Brighton 'E4' class 0-6-2Ts used throughout the 1950s. Maunsell's 'Q' class 0-6-0 was his final design, introduced in 1938, mainly to replace earlier goods engines, though they also regularly appeared on various passenger duties. Several had front-end modifications from 1958 onwards, including No 30547, to overcome steaming difficulties found prevalent from the earliest days with the type.

Former LBSCR 'K' class 2-6-0 No 32345 is shown here at Beeding cement works on 28 April 1962 with one of the last duties regularly allocated to these engines. This short section, north of Shoreham, on the branch to Christ's Hospital, was ultimately closed to traffic in May 1980, when replacement by road haulage took effect.

The 'K' class, eventually numbering 17 engines, was introduced by Chief Engineer Lawson Billinton in 1913 for express goods work, and these were, at the time, the most powerful on the system. They proved their worth in handling the additional amount of freight traffic brought about by World War 1.

It had been the intention to follow this design with a similar one for an express goods tank engine, to be known as Class K2, with a 2-6-2 wheel arrangement. However, the proposal was later cancelled, and a further seven 'K' class (later BR Nos 32347-53) were constructed instead, in 1920/21.

Following the Grouping and formation of the Southern Railway, the cab profile was altered and dome flattened, to suit the composite loading gauge applying over the whole system. A shortened chimney was also provided.

Regrettably, no example of these useful and handsome engines was preserved, despite earlier hopes, the whole class having been withdrawn at the end of 1962, still with many years of effective life. *G. Daniels*

*Left:* Late on an autumn afternoon, on 3 November 1963, earlier and later modified examples of 'Q' class 0-6-0s, Nos 30543 and 30531, proceed along the Lavant branch with a railtour. This was the remaining section of line between Chichester and Midhurst, closed to passengers in 1935. After progressive freight closures south of Midhurst between 1951 and 1953, Lavant became the railhead for sugar beet and finally aggregates traffic, itself closing in March 1991.

*Above:* Standing outside Feltham (70B) shed, close to Heathrow airport as shown by the Boeing 707 jet visible above the tender in the foreground (!), we find, on 25 March 1962, 'G16' class 4-8-0T No 30495 and 'H16' class 4-6-2T No 30520.

Both types were introduced in 1921 by LSWR CME Robert Urie specifically for use at the then newly-opened Feltham hump marshalling yard. The four 'G16's were for shunting and handling of goods transfer traffic to Nine Elms, whilst the five 'H16's were to be employed on similar transfer work to and from Willesden (LNWR) and Brent (MR) yards. The former, with their near 34,000lb tractive effort, were considered the country's most powerful tank engines. Later 'H16' work included ECS duties between Clapham Junction and Waterloo around 1959, whilst in 1960 two were allocated to Eastleigh for Fawley oil tank trains. Final withdrawals of both types came in 1962. *K. W. Wightman*

*Above:* Amongst veteran engines on BR during the 1950s were examples of the LSWR '0395' class 0-6-0 goods engines, introduced by William Adams from 1881. These had latterly been numbered in the company's duplicate list. Some were used overseas by the Railway Operating Division (ROD) in World War 1, four being sunk in transit on the torpedoed SS *Arabic*. Eighteen survived into BR service, renumbered 30564-81. No 30567 (SR 3154) was the last remaining, being withdrawn in September 1959. With an ex-LCDR boiler, it is seen here at Feltham, its long-time home, on 20 June 1959. *T. B. Owen*

*Right:* Against the familiar background of Windsor Castle, 'U' class 2-6-0s Nos 31791 and 31639 head the return RCTS 'Longmoor' railtour from Windsor & Eton Riverside on 30 April 1966. Part of the line passes through Crown property and required Royal assent. Electrification was completed in July 1930.

Following their displacement from the Lyme Regis branch, on which the type had reigned supreme since 1913, the three remaining engines of the former LSWR '0415' class 4-4-2Ts were withdrawn from service. They were the only type, following modification, which had been found particularly suitable for the lines twisting nature and the severity of its ruling 1-in-40 gradients. A variety of trials were carried out over the years, latterly even including the former GWR '14xx' class 0-4-2Ts, following the Western Region takeover of lines west of Salisbury in January 1963. Prior to the arrival of the '0415' engines, former LBSCR 'A1' class 0-6-0Ts and 'O2' class 0-4-4Ts had been used, but were unable to cope with the line's topography. Only two engines were originally retained to work it, and a motive power shortage in the postwar period forced the Southern Railway to look elsewhere. Fortunately, a further example, former LSWR No 488, still existed on the East Kent Railway as their No 5. This had

come to them in 1919 via the Government's Ridham General Salvage Depot at Sittingbourne, which had purchased it from the LSWR in 1917. The company was, consequently, able to reacquire it in 1946, when it was given the Duplicate List number 3488. As chance would have it, this is the one engine that now survives, having been preserved at the Bluebell Railway under its original LSWR identity. There were originally some 71 examples of the class, these having been constructed in batches by such builders as Beyer Peacock, Neilson, etc., between 1882 and 1885. Designed by William Adams, they were intended for working suburban services, and became quickly redundant following electrification, the majority being withdrawn in the 1920s. In 1961 it was found possible to replace them with Ivatt Class 2MT 2-6-2Ts, and the REC 'LSWR Suburban Lines' railtour provided the opportunity to return No 30582 to its former haunts on 19 March 1961. The train is seen standing alongside Guildford South signalbox.

A unique winter view of 'D' class 4-4-0 No 31577, designed by SECR Locomotive Superintendent Harry Wainwright, with a Birdcage Triple set of former SECR coaches, near North Camp, whilst working a Reading to Redhill local service on 10 March 1956. The combination had been a familiar sight, particularly in the postwar era, on this stretch of line, and was due to disappear permanently by the following December, when the last two examples, No 31075 and that illustrated, were taken out of service. The three coach rakes, which had been used on the line since, at least, the early-1930s, similarly vanished around 1960.

The 'D' class was considered by many to be the epitome of handsome Victorian express 4-4-0 design, and No 737 (BR No 31737) was restored to its original SECR lined-green splendour following withdrawal. It now forms part of the National Railway Museum collection at York.

A number of the 51 examples built were constructed by outside contractors, such as Stephenson and Sharp Stewart, but No 31577 was built at Ashford in 1906. The first deliveries took place in 1901, and No 735 (BR No 31735) was exhibited in the Glasgow Exhibition of that year. However, it was amongst the first of the class to be rebuilt by Maunsell to 'D1' standard, this taking place at the Gorton works of Beyer Peacock in 1921.

The combination illustrated was later replaced, for a time, by newly-built BR Standard Class 4MT 2-6-0s, and subsequently by various Maunsell Moguls, hauling his narrow-bodied coaches.
*T. B. Owen*

*Left:* 'Schools' class 4-4-0 No 30903 *Charterhouse* heads towards Guildford, near Farnborough North, with a working from Reading South on 22 September 1962. The line was opened between these points as part of the Reading, Guildford & Reigate Railway, incorporated in 1846. The line traversed much of rural Hampshire and Surrey, being noted for its scenic nature and following the North Downs ridge between Guildford and Reigate. The latter section was initially proposed for passenger closure in the 1963 Beeching Plan, but now hosts a well-patronised DMU service between Reading and Gatwick Airport. The line has also been considered to provide an Outer London freight link for Channel Tunnel traffic. The 'Schools' were introduced to the line on a regular basis in

1960, mainly as a result of redundancy in Kent following the modernisation schemes of the late 1950s. *A. A. Jarvis*

*Above:* The down 'Bournemouth Belle' approaches Alton station on a Sunday during March 1966, hauled by rebuilt 'WC' class 4-6-2 No 34017 *Ilfracombe*. During Bournemouth-line electrification works a number of weekend diversions were arranged over the Mid-Hants line between Alton and Winchester, many taking place during the winter of 1966. The route was known to enginemen as 'Over the Alps' due to its taxing gradients either side of Medstead & Four Marks.

*Above:* In a rather wintry scene 'U' class 2-6-0 No 31639 stands at Bordon station with the second LCGB 'S15 Commemorative' railtour on 16 January 1966. It had taken over from 'S15' No 30837 at the branch junction of Bentley, enabling a final trip over the line. This had lost its passenger services on 16 September 1957, finally closing to freight on 4 April 1966.

*Right:* Rebuilt 'MN' class 4-6-2 No 35004 *Cunard White Star* clears its cylinders after recovering from a check at Pirbright during October 1964, whilst in charge of a

Bournemouth to Waterloo express. Built in 1941 as No 21C4, it was rebuilt to the condition shown in July 1958, the complete class being dealt with between 1956 and 1959. Bulleid Pacifics of all types became predominant on Bournemouth workings following the demise of the 'Lord Nelsons' in 1962, and remained until electrification of the route was completed in July 1967 and steam power finally eliminated from the Region. The final weeks included some outstanding performances when the magic 100mph was exceeded.

'Q1' class 0-6-0 No 33006 moves away from Hook station on a frosty Sunday morning in December 1965 with an engineering spoil train, whilst work is carried out in connection with the Bournemouth line electrification programme. The 'Q1s' were introduced by CME O. V. S. Bulleid in 1942 to provide an especially powerful freight locomotive to supplement the existing fleet of 0-6-0s, most of which were of pre-Grouping origin. Their particularly unorthodox appearance was partly the result of wartime restrictions on the use of materials. However, they proved an extremely useful addition to the existing fleet, the class eventually totalling some 40 examples. They were particularly popular with locomotive crews, amongst which they gained the affectionate nickname of 'Charlies', possibly arising from the 'C' prefix used in SR days (eg C6 in this case) for the engine identity under Bulleid's original numbering scheme.

Approaching Basingstoke, past a fine GWR bracket signal, on the line from Reading which had come under Southern Region control from 1950, 'LN' class 4-6-0 No 30860 *Lord Hawke* heads a train from York to Bournemouth on 9 May 1959. This would have been a regular working for Southern engines, these usually taking over such trains at Oxford on the Western Region. *K. W. Wightman*

*Above:* Following Dugald Drummond's appointment as LSWR Locomotive Superintendent, an order was placed on Dübs of Glasgow in 1897 for 30 0-6-0 goods engines, to be known as the '700' class. These were basically similar to his CR '340' class ('Jumbos') of the 1880s. During 1921 successor Robert Urie decided on a rebuild programme, with a higher pitched boiler, increased cylinder diameter and pressure raised from 175 to 180psi. An extended smokebox was fitted and front end lengthened to suit. No 30368 is seen running light at Basingstoke on 20 March 1957. *T. B. Owen*

*Right:* The 'Lord Nelson' ('LN') class 4-6-0s were introduced by Maunsell in August 1926 to meet management requirements, expressed in 1923, for a locomotive capable of hauling trains of 500 tons tare over the main routes at average speeds of around 55mph. However, this was a difficult target to attain, and they were less than wholly successful initially despite various modifications. Performance was found especially variable on the West of England services. When Bulleid took over from Maunsell in 1937 he decided to embody principles which had first been proven in France. Chief among these was the installation of the Lemaitre multi-jet blastpipe, together with improvements in cylinder design and piston valves of increased diameter. Their capabilities were considerably improved and, had it not been for the intervention of World War 2, acceleration of the Bournemouth services, on which they were prominent, would probably have been initiated earlier. In this view No 30865 *Sir John Hawkins* is shown at Basingstoke with a Bournemouth to Waterloo semi-fast on 2 March 1957. *K. W. Wightman*

51

*Left:* One of the last few remaining Adams LSWR dock tanks, 'B4' class 0-4-0T No 30096, is seen here alongside the River Itchen and on the DNSR line close to Shawford Junction, with a railtour to Southampton Docks on 6 April 1963. The 'B4' class, including Drummond examples, totalled 25, the first appearing in 1891. Another duty included that at Winchester (SR) goods yard due to severe siding curvature. All had disappeared by October 1963.

*Above:* The Southern, in addition to its regular fleet, also owned a variety of elderly tank engines used on shunting duties in the various engineering depots around the system. These were included in a separate Departmental Stock list.

One such is illustrated here at Eastleigh MPD on 18 May 1963, shortly before cutting-up. Former LSWR 'G6' class 0-6-0T No DS682 (previously No 30238) had been based at the Meldon ballast quarry in Devon from November 1960, where it had replaced an earlier engine of the same class. It was itself succeeded by 'USA' class 0-6-0T No DS234 (BR No 30062) in December 1962, when withdrawal took place. No DS682 was the final example in service, those in capital stock all having been condemned by November 1961. The class of 34 engines was introduced by William Adams in 1894 for short-distance goods work and shunting duties, being a six-coupled version of the 'O2' class 0-4-4Ts.

Depicted here in a view taken on 9 October 1966, rebuilt 'BB' class 4-6-2 No 34052 passes Romsey's LSWR signalbox on its journey to Salisbury with the Southern Counties Touring Society (SCTS) 'Four Counties' railtour. The engine had been named *Lord Dowding*, but the nameplates have been taken away, probably to counter the possibility of premature illegal removal, which was prevalent across the BR system towards the close of the steam era. The tracks deviating to the right towards Southampton, via Nursling, now form the main route from the Salisbury direction. This had been one of those selected for a pilot scheme, employing diesel multiple-units on a fixed interval basis during 1957, and still carries regular freight traffic between Southampton and other former BR regions, along with similar through passenger workings. The original main line from Romsey to Eastleigh, via Chandlers Ford, is now maintained solely as a freight link. *D. B. Clark*

The line between Andover and Romsey was opened by the LSWR during March 1865. It became derisively identified as the 'sprat and winkle' line, which probably originated from its coastal associations and the 'SWR' initials borne by some locomotives. In June 1885 a connection was opened from Fullerton Junction to Hurstbourne on the West of England main line. However, passenger traffic was always limited, and ceased on 6 July 1931. The main route was also closed to all traffic on 7 September 1964. 'Q' class 0-6-0 No 30548 is seen at a somewhat run-down Fullerton Junction with a railtour on 18 April 1964.

*Left:* A scene in Southampton Docks in March 1962 with 'USA' class 0-6-0T No 30068 shunting Maunsell FK coach No S7406S, a type associated with the Ocean Liner expresses. The class, designed by the US Army Transportation Corps for use in Europe after D-Day, was obtained by the SR in 1946 to replace the ageing 'B4' class 0-4-0Ts. A few survived, of the 14 purchased, to enter Departmental service when dieselisation came in the 1960s. *L. F. Folkard*

*Above:* Shown crossing Canute Road in the Southampton Docks area on 19 September 1962, Maunsell 'S15' class 4-6-0 No 30839 is seen with a fine line-up of cars of the period. The locomotive headcode denotes 'Light engines

from all stations west of Basingstoke to Eastleigh', and it may be returning after working a freight to the dock area. The class was introduced on the LSWR in 1920 by Robert Urie for fast freight and heavy passenger traffic. Twenty examples were built (BR Nos 30496-515), based on his 'N15' design but with smaller coupled wheels. Maunsell added a further 25 engines (BR Nos 30823-47) between 1927 and 1936. A number were acquired by the preservation movement, two Urie examples (Nos 30499 and 30506) now being on the Mid-Hants Railway. Maunsell engines are currently located at Swanage, Goathland and Sheffield Park. *A. A. Jarvis*

Former LBSCR 'E2' class 0-6-0T No 32104 is depicted here engaged in a shunting movement in Southampton Docks in March 1962. The wooden-bodied wagons involved are probably Departmental Engineers' stock. The class, which eventually comprised some 10 examples, was the initial design of Chief Locomotive Engineer Lawson Billinton, first appearing in 1913. They were produced for goods traffic and shunting work, and to supersede earlier examples of the 'E1' class 0-6-0Ts. However, the example illustrated is of particular interest, as, along with LBSCR No 103 (BR No 32103), it was modified in 1914 to enable the operation of a six-coach push-pull unit between London Bridge and Crystal Palace. In the event, these trials did not prove successful and were abandoned after a short period. The last five constructed (BR Nos 32105-9) differed from the earlier examples in having a front extension to their side tanks allowing a significant increase in water capacity. In their final years four were allocated to Southampton Docks, whilst the remainder were split between Norwood Junction (2) and Stewarts Lane (4) depots. All were withdrawn by April 1963. *L. F. Folkard*

Crossing the well-known Medina Bridge, on the outskirts of Newport station, with a Cowes-bound working, 'O2' class 0-4-4T No W16 *Ventnor* is shown hauling its train of pre-Grouping coaching stock during August 1965. Though not immediately apparent, the left-hand bridge span is, in fact, moveable, though disused at the time of the photograph. Apart from its locomotives, the Isle of Wight system was also distinctive in operating various coaches which had become redundant on the mainland, these being during the last years, mainly of LBSCR and SECR origin. All were eliminated with electrification in March 1967.

The Isle of Wight, with its pre-Grouping engines and coaches, was a firm favourite with enthusiasts, especially in later years when the majority of such stock had disappeared from the mainland system. During early 1960 plans had been drawn up to replace the elderly 'O2' class locomotives with BR Standard Class 2MT 2-6-2Ts in the 84xxx series. To meet gauge limitations, these would have been modified at Eastleigh by fitting a new chimney over 6in shorter, reducing dome and cab height and removing the cab side screens. However, the scheme was later abandoned, no alterations having taken place, and it was eventually decided to proceed with electrification. Once again, redundant rolling stock (!) would be used, this time from the London Underground system, due to weight and other local restrictions. Steam operations finally ended in December 1966, when the remaining Ryde to Shanklin section closed to enable the necessary work to be completed. The line from Shanklin onwards to Ventnor had already ceased operation the previous April. Reopening of the now-electrified system took place in March 1967. Former LSWR 'O2' class 0-4-4T No W17 *Seaview* is seen here climbing Apse Bank with a Ventnor train in August 1965, shortly after leaving Shanklin.

In a New Forest location close to Lymington Junction, former LSWR 'M7' class 0-4-4T No 30048 passes over an occupation crossing, on the loop line via Ringwood, with a Bournemouth to Brockenhurst auto working during August 1963. Of interest is the standard goods brake van, unusually coupled between the locomotive and its Maunsell push-pull set. The route was initially the main line to Christchurch, via Hurn, before opening of the direct line via Sway. Closed to all traffic east of Ringwood on 4 May 1964, the double-track line had been a useful diversionary route when the main line came under maintenance, and its loss was much lamented. The 'M7' class, originally 105 strong, was Drummond's initial design, first appearing in 1897. They were the most common locomotives of their type on the LSWR, and several were adapted for push-pull duties. In April 1923 No 58 (BR No 30058) achieved fame by hauling a Royal train of three ordinary coaches from Waterloo to Bookham, conveying the Duke and Duchess of York on the first stage of their honeymoon. No 672 was involved in a bizarre shunting incident in May 1948, when it was drawn into a Waterloo & City Line lift shaft at Waterloo, being subsequently dismantled on site. *L. F. Folkard*

As already noted, Ringwood was the junction for the line to Christchurch via Hurn until its complete closure in September 1935. Following withdrawal of passenger services from the remaining Broadstone to Brockenhurst line on 4 May 1964, it became the eastern limit for freight working, before this was again cut back to Wimborne on 7 September 1967. Prior to this taking effect the line was visited by the BYTS 'Hampshire Explorer' railtour, shown here on 21 May 1966, hauled by unrebuilt 'WC' Pacific No 34006 *Bude*. It will be seen that the station nameboard has already been relieved of its individually cast lettering produced at the company's Exmouth Junction concrete works. No 34006, which took part in the original BR 1948 Locomotive Exchanges, is also noteworthy as having worked, with No 34057 *Biggin Hill*, the final railtour over the SDJR system in March 1966 before complete closure. Services to Wimborne finally ceased on 13 May 1977, whilst the trackbed from there to Ringwood was incorporated into the Ferndown by-pass (A31) road. *D. B. Clark*

One of the lesser-known byways of the system was that which ran from Salisbury (Alderbury Junction) to West Moors. It had been opened on 20 December 1866 by the Salisbury & Dorset Junction Railway, the LSWR taking over operations in 1883. With a rather sparse passenger service, the line inevitably closed to all traffic on 4 May 1964, the long-unrenovated stations remaining in something of an LSWR time warp until closure. In this scene SR 'N' class 2-6-0 No 31404 is shown engaged in shunting at Verwood with the 5.32pm Wimborne to Salisbury (East Yard) freight on 6 July 1961. *John Langford*

*Left:* In this view, taken at Swanage on 20 August 1966, BR Standard Class 4MT 2-6-4T No 80019 marshalls its two branch coaches, whilst sister engine No 80011 waits to couple onto its main-line holiday train, which will probably attach to a Weymouth to Waterloo service at Wareham. As the older Southern types vanished from the scene, they gave way to the BR Standard '4MT' and LMR '2MT' tanks, which then became the usual power here.

*Above:* The first significant conventional line on the Isle of Portland was the Weymouth & Portland Railway, which opened on 16 October 1865. The Easton & Church Hope Railway, authorised in 1867, subsequently opened to goods,

especially stone traffic, on 1 October 1900, and to passengers on 1 September 1902. Meanwhile, the Admiralty-owned Breakwater Railway had started operation in 1878. This was used to join the gap between the two companies. The combined lines were jointly worked by the GWR and LSWR, an intensive railmotor service being introduced in 1910 from Melcombe Regis, opened 1909, just short of the junction with the main line. With population decline in the postwar period passenger services ended on 3 March 1952, freight following on 5 April 1965. 'M7' class 0-4-4T No 30107 is pictured at Easton with an enthusiasts' special on 7 June 1958. *T. B. Owen*

A general view of the west end of Salisbury station on 8 August 1963, with rebuilt 'BB' class 4-6-2 No 34060 *25 Squadron* heading a West of England service, whilst one-time WR '57xx' class 0-6-0PT No 4626 undertakes station pilot duties. Salisbury was an important junction on the former LSWR, serving routes to London, Exeter and beyond, Southampton via Romsey and the branch via Fordingbridge to Bournemouth, together with GWR traffic from the Westbury direction. The GWR originally boasted its own station at Salisbury (Fisherton), together with adjacent three-road locomotive shed (SAL). This facility closed in September 1932 whilst the shed lasted until 1950. Their former site on the extreme left, now being home to SouthWest Trains maintenance depot. Salisbury station layout otherwise remains substantially unchanged, although the Southern MPD, closed in June 1967, was later demolished.
*D. B. Clark*

At Templecombe, on the crossroads of the Somerset & Dorset line from Bath to Bournemouth and the Southern's West of England main line between Salisbury and Exeter, we find 'N' class 2-6-0 No 31855, which has taken over the final 7.00am Cleethorpes to Exmouth and Sidmouth service, via the SDJR, on 1 September 1962. Also visible is named BR Standard Class 5MT 4-6-0 No 73088 *Joyous Gard* with the 3.41pm Templecombe to Exeter stopping service.

Following the WR takeover of the former SR main line west of Salisbury in January 1963 most of the route was singled and reduced to secondary status. Templecombe (SR) station itself closed with the end of SDJR services in March 1966, but, following public pressure, reopened to passengers in October 1983, with the signalbox initially doubling as a ticket office and waiting room. Exeter and Waterloo services now call here using its solitary platform. *A. A. Jarvis*

*Left:* On a blisteringly hot spring afternoon in May 1964, rebuilt 'MN' class 4-6-2 No 35012 *United States Lines* is shown shortly after leaving Yeovil Junction with a Waterloo service. On 13 June 1964 No 35012 worked a noteworthy enthusiasts special, the 'Solway Ranger', from Leeds to Carlisle and return, over both Shap and Ais Gill summits. With Southern driver Bert Hooker in charge, some excellent performances were recorded with the nine-coach train despite operating problems. On 24 April 1953 a serious failure at Crewkerne, when unrebuilt 'MN' class No 35020 *Bibby Line* on a Waterloo service suffered a crank axle fracture, led to the temporary withdrawal of the whole class. Motive power was rapidly borrowed, including 'V2' 2-6-2s and 'B1' 4-6-0s from the ER

along with Class '5' 4-6-0s and 'Britannia' 4-6-2s from the LMR. These were all returned by that July. Steam west of Salisbury officially ended on 6 September 1964.

*Above:* Yeovil Junction, on the Waterloo to Exeter main line, was around two miles from the town centre, and a connection to Yeovil Town station was provided by a regular shuttle service. 'M7' class 0-4-4T No 30131 with its two-coach set approaches Town station from Yeovil Junction on 13 June 1958. This service ceased operation on 2 October 1966. The line to Yeovil (Pen Mill) can be seen diverging in the background. *T. B. Owen*

*Above:* A broad view here in May 1964 of Yeovil Town shed, by now under WR control, with a variety of BR Standard, Southern and GWR locos evident. The latter's presence resulted from the earlier Pen Mill depot closure in 1959, all duties being transferred. Evidence of the 1963 WR takeover is indicated by the '64xx' class 0-6-0PT, just visible towards the picture centre, on the Yeovil Junction shuttle service, the type having replaced the 'M7' class on these workings. The shed, which had been built around 1861, was closed in June 1965, after which the whole area was cleared to provide a large town car park.

Following closure of the direct route between here and Pen Mill station, it became an official public footpath.

*Right:* BR Standard Class 4MT 2-6-4T No 80041 slowly approaches the River Otter bridge, near Tipton St Johns, with its two-coach set from Exmouth via Budleigh Salterton in February 1965. The steeply graded ascent to Sidmouth can be seen in the foreground. Standard classes partly replaced the 'M7s' and 'O2s' from the early 1950s. *T. B. Owen*

32135

*Left:* Ten LBSCR 'E1' class 0-6-0Ts were rebuilt by Maunsell from 1927 as 'E1R' class 0-6-2Ts, with a radial trailing truck. Allowing increased coal capacity, this provided a suitable engine for work on steeply graded West Country branches, especially that between Halwill and Torrington. Final duties were banking at Exeter, and No 32135 is illustrated at Exmouth Junction depot on 5 July 1957. *R.C. Riley*

*Above:* As an unidentified rebuilt Bulleid Light Pacific descends the 1-in-37 bank from Exeter Central to Exeter St Davids with a westbound service in August 1962, 'Z' class 0-8-0T No 30956 gives rear-end assistance to a train in the opposite direction. The coaches are, unusually, in standard lined maroon livery, rather than Southern Region green. The three-cylinder 'Z' class was introduced by Maunsell in 1929 to provide a powerful engine for use in hump and other marshalling yards, and possessed sufficient side play at leading and trailing wheels to negotiate $4\frac{1}{2}$ chain curves. The complete class of eight engines, built at Brighton, ended their days at Exeter on banking duties, being replaced in autumn 1962, due to excessive boiler wear, by the 'W' class 2-6-4Ts. *T. J. Edgington*

*Above:* Former LSWR Drummond 'T9' class 4-4-0 No 30717, on a down stopping service, is shown at Meldon Quarry staff platform on 19 July 1958, allowing an enthusiast party to alight for a works visit. Class sister No 30120 was secured for preservation and is currently on the Bluebell Railway. *T. B. Owen*

*Right:* Probably the most well-known engineering feat on the former LSWR lines west of Exeter is the 120ft-high Meldon Viaduct on the Okehampton to Plymouth route. It was originally built in 1874 for single track only, but a second structure was interlaced with the first in 1879, allowing the use of double track.

Following route closure between Okehampton and Bere Alston in May 1968, it served initially as a quarry headshunt, but has since found a new role as a Dartmoor footpath and cycleway. A Bulleid Light Pacific crosses the West Okement valley on 19 July 1958 with a Plymouth working. *T. B. Owen*

*Left:* The Callington branch was owned and worked independently by the Plymouth, Devonport & South Western Junction Railway (PDSWJR), which took over from the, originally narrow gauge, East Cornwall Mineral Railway in 1891, the line being extended across Calstock Viaduct to Bere Alston in 1908. Mineral traffic declined between the wars when market garden produce took over, and at the line's peak in the 1950s, double-heading of the mixed trains carrying fruit and flowers was frequently required. Former LSWR 'O2' class 0-4-4T No 30192, its burnt smokebox showing evidence of hard work along this steeply graded branch, is shown approaching the terminus on 20 June 1958. The two push-pull coaches are of former LSWR gate stock, access being by decorative wrought-iron gates in each carriage centre. *T. B. Owen*

*Above:* To operate the Callington line the PDSWJR obtained an 0-6-0T and two 0-6-2Ts from Hawthorn, Leslie of Newcastle in 1907. These were absorbed by the Southern and eventually became BR Nos 30756-8. Replaced by the LSWR 'O2s' they were later used at Plymouth on local duties. No 30757 *Earl of Mount Edgcumbe* is shown at Eastleigh on 30 March 1957, the year of its withdrawal. *T. B. Owen*

77

The Halwill Junction to Torrington line was opened by the Southern on 27 July 1925, mainly to serve china clay workings in the Meeth area, the first six miles from Torrington replacing a 3ft gauge mineral tramway, built in 1880, to the Marland works of the North Devon Clay Company. Passenger traffic was always sparse and ended on 1 March 1965, the line remaining open for china clay traffic between Meeth and Barnstaple Junction. A final railtour was arranged over the complete route on 27 March 1965, staff being retained especially to man the previously closed section. The 'Exmoor Ranger', a joint PRC/RCTS venture, was hauled by LMR '2MT' class 2-6-2Ts Nos 41206 and 41291. The leading engine is seen here crossing the A386 road on its approach to Meeth Halt, where the isolated and twisting nature of the line is well evident. Formal closure of the remaining section to all traffic took effect on 8 November 1982.

Engaged in shunting at Boscarne Junction on 4 May 1964, 'N' class 2-6-0 No 31840 is seen with a short van train. Boscarne Junction adjoined the exchange sidings of the freight only branch along which the ancient Beattie well tanks worked china clay trains from Wenford Bridge, until replacement by GWR '1366' class 0-6-0PTs in 1962. The line closed officially to all traffic in November 1983.

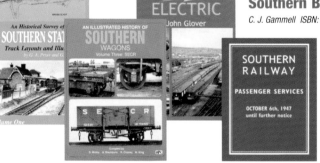